SINGING IN THE DARK TIMES

SINGING IN THE DARK TIMES

MARGARET CORVID

PATRICIAN PRESS
MANNINGTREE

First published as a paperback edition by Patrician Press 2022

British Library Cataloguing in Publication Data. A catalogue record for this book is available from the British Library.

ISBN paperback edition 978-1-8380598-4-2

Published by Patrician Press Collective 2022

For Nila — may they be a light in other worlds

Dos lid hot geshribn iz mit blut un nit mit blay'

*This lied (song) was written with blood and not
with lead.*

From the Yiddish partisan song Zog Nit
Keynmol by Hersch Glick

Contents

INTRODUCTION

Margaret Corvid has been writing for many years, but this is her first published poetry collection. My publisher, Patrician Press, asked me to take a first look at the collection and give an opinion. From experience, I do not begin such a task with any great expectations. Too often, the ambition runs ahead of the achievement. Margaret is a political activist and journalist but has recently returned to poetry, influenced and encouraged by her friend, the poet Roz Kaveney.

A recent bulletin of the Poetry Book Society lists more than 50 new titles, so it is a crowded field and the jostle for attention from readers involves the writer in competition with established and new poets, accomplished and not, modernist and traditional. Armitage is there, Crichton-Smith and Ashbery as well as many you won't have heard of. And some you won't hear of again.

Margaret Corvid you will hear of again, I am sure. I read the first poem in the collection, 'Siena', a lament about Covid-19, with mounting excitement, partly induced by the relentless, unpunctuated pace, but also by the confidence, innovation and intelligibility of the poem. And the sudden epiphanies: 'hasty sips of breath' stopped me in my tracks, headlong though my pace was. 'Hospitals in frightful battle dress' another striking moment. The poem also has a confident and easy structure which is not straightforward with punctuation eschewed.

Poets often place the best of their poems first or last in their collections, so you might expect the second to be a let-down. 'Jo Cox' though is far from that: it's a sad and savage subject but Margaret pulls it off 'Your neighbours are at war with you, you know' a sinister refrain.

Two adjacent sonnets (her favoured form) offer interesting evidence of Margaret's variety and versatility. 'The Ass of my Anxiety' and 'Red Flags': the first with a chaos of imagery, meaning dancing slightly out of sight, but bright and exciting, and the second a sombre story of a controlling stranger. Both are technically accomplished, both strongly felt and persuasive.

There is a frankness and honesty about the poems which is very likeable. Margaret's heart is on show: her views and her feelings on display. You take them or leave them: it's up to you.

Above all, there is a variety and exuberance in the collection, verve in the subject matter and competence technically.

It would be startling if Margaret were able to maintain this high standard throughout the collection, and it is true some poems do fall slightly short and some baffle a little, but this would also be true of many respected poets. A little bafflement can offer an interesting challenge after all. Sometimes a poem will stretch for a pinnacle but collapse into bathos. Margaret is an intelligent writer, so I'm sure if she continues to write poetry, as I hope she will, her work will reach even higher peaks, and avoid the crevasses awaiting the rash.

Martin Johnson

Author of *Robert Macfarlane's Orphans*

SIENA

And while Siena sleeps, the streetlamps glow
all yellow in the misty quiet night
and shine upon the empty streets below
a melody is rising with the light

deliberate and clear as if performed
by someone who had learned it at the knee
of grandmothers who cherished held and warned
of what had passed and what would come to be

invisible and ravaging in weeks
the hacking cough and hasty sips of breath
the ghostly crows that carried in their beaks
our graceful singing in the face of death

the harmonies that gather with the strength
of tenements all washed with cups of wine
the slam of footballs hard against the fence
the laundry, white, a-flutter on the line

the hospitals in frightful battle dress
beholden to the dead for all their gold
the empty churches, nothing to confess
both overlook the sickly and the old

the tram to work, the frightened eyes and masks
and every word and breath and rasping sound
life giving ichor bubbling in its flasks
discarded prayers, abandoned and unwound

and while Siena sleeps, or can't, it tries
to rally round the heartbeat of the age
an ancient folk song never truly dies
and as the reaper waits for us backstage

full-voiced, sung with a curse or blessing found
to all our fathers buried in the ground.

JO COX

Your neighbours are at war with you, you know.
Their gardens flower brightly as their hate.
So quietly they try to seize the state,
spin it awry, knocked to their hateful flow.

I'm just a poet, no Cassandra me,
no screaming pilot voice to steer us clear.
Frankly, I've shit myself from just the fear
I've got here just in time to be unfree,

a howling werewolf running down the hate.
She died, I sobbed, and puffy eyed I worked
and mumbled bullshit to the random jerk
that hired me. Then I wept, and slept, and ate.

And while I sleep the hate and gardens grow.
Your neighbours are at war with you, you know.

NEVER AGAIN

They hid the scrolls and scattered to the wind
all sly like russet foxes leapt the fence
and paid blood, tears and passports, fifty pence
and memories. But if the tale begins

in cattle cars, speed the division true
and lined up for the gas, recorded right
and murdered in nine hundred bloody nights
only by chance it wasn't me or you.

The luck of dice, only the morning call
alarm bells, lined in squares, a single case.
What is a name? A privilege and a place
all signed away. Together, we did fall

and shattered, with a single stroke of pen
together, sing, and pray: Never again.

CLASS CONSCIOUSNESS

We learn it's not our fault that we're afraid.
We learn our terrors burst from every breast
and nurse our wounds, pare rot with wicked blade.
The monsters walk the earth in human flesh,

and build machines, bureaucracy and war
to spare their ears from all the piercing screams,
to spare their hands from plunging in the gore.
We learn to watch, to spot the hidden seams,

the flesh lines, stitching skin to stolen skin,
each demon muscle swathed in baby fat.
We learn we're raised for slaughter, that to win
is our dead faces, flayed off, stretched flat

and cured, and honoured, hung on castle walls,
mouths stuffed with praise: we never lived at all.

CORONA PESACH

How is this night unlike all other nights
when snuck in passages we go to pray?
The lace cloth, burnt egg brown and speckled white,
our worship in our rooms, all locked away,

the butcher's brisket wrapped and hurried home,
the matzo standing watch upon the shelves,
the candles lit for blessings made alone,
trembling in awe and fear, wrapped round ourselves.

How is this night unlike all other nights?
In prayer our voices rise, each in its part.
Next year together, hope with all our might,
next year in the Jerusalem of hearts,

but now the breaths of ventilators rush
to greet the souls all gathered in the hush.

SMALL

We cannot small our way into respect.
We cannot whisper, copying the voice
of women who have never had a choice
and soft spoken, and gentle, indirect

ask for a shred of light, of life, of ease
and childlike, like an old Disney cartoon
open the window, gaze up at the moon
and wait for fairies, hours upon our knees.

We cannot cram ourselves into a box
and hear the package tape seal up our ears
load on the train, all trembling with our fear
and wait till someone opens up the locks

and wipes us clean, to sit on heaven's shelf:
We'll have to stitch our lives from life itself.

OUR REVOLUTION

Let it have no known leader, this campaign.
Let it be led by cool fresh water, clear and sweet,
follow the ringing out, we, across the tunnel walls to light,
backs straightened, blinking in the rain.

Let land lead it, green and brown, down to the grey of rock,
no borders known, remembering anciently
when the water joined all grounds, the primeval talk,
forged in liquid fire. Slowly and patiently

lands grew closer, apart. Let dinosaurs lead it,
flying, jumping fences in a breath.
Let us sacrifice the steer, hoist it up and bleed it,
all take a mouthful of its succulent death.

Look behind us, and call this the festival times
when flags and bunting fade, tacked to the bricks,
and let the children mock us in nursery rhymes,
weaving loose springy baskets from the greenest sticks,

remembering the day we snatched ourselves up,
and, shivering, turned away from the abyss.

BRISTOL

Let us melt the statues down
weigh them out on starlight scales,
lop off all the horses' tails,
hang the swords as chandeliers,

brush rifles aside in fear,
sail across a thousand harbours,
let us give our children water,
horns of plenty, ruby crowns.

Let us throw the prisons open
all unlocked in silent prayer,
picks and files tucked in our hair,
walk among the idols broken

up in hope, remembering
the first words that God ever spoke,
when bonds of iron and money broke
the harbour waters, trembling.

SUPERMOON

The supermoon draws timeless cords towards earth,
not timeless? close enough, and earth pulls towards
the moon, and lifts a hundred leaping boards,
a million fish, all sparkled diamonds worth

a lightyear ship dismantled by the cloud
and built again when strands of mist disperse.
Fifty years back it did the same and worse:
your girlish neck drawn taut and shoulders proud

through smoke and sirens, marching towards the moon,
as yellow as a shining golden plate,
no? Close enough. The hunt departs in state
and will not scourge again anytime soon,

you said. The titan and his young play rough,
hate basking in the light, no? Close enough.

CORONA REQUIEM

From all angers, pulses confidential
on the monitors, and all the beeps,
pray to die within your blessed sleep,
all the bread and oranges essential,

all the wishes, sorries, thanks and hopes,
all appreciations, all applause,
all the sunbathers outside the laws,
all the empty easters, all the popes,

from all blessed angers, tombs that open
all the drowning gasps from underground,
in their mourning, gathering the sound
all the chanting vigils, voices broken

asking how they carry, torn and mangled,
empty sepulchres, from all their angers.

SCHOOL

I was just little when they killed my 'me'.
I never had it, just a ragged hole.
They don't teach you in school, but every soul
is held on by a twig. You pop it free

With just a little press, stem breaks away.
The soul takes on a waxy sheen. They don't
teach you this stuff in school. If asked, they say
the words printed on old cards. If they won't

cast eyes on children sitting at the back
with empty places tucked behind their hearts,
they know. The kind that dress each day in black
and draw the empty spot in lesson books. In art

I whispered, but to speak of it is cruel.
So many things they don't teach you in school.

PAPER DOLLS

They stole my paper dolls from me
and said they were cut out too fine,
too small, obsession. Over tea
they spilled across my family line,

and every picture perfectly
erased by fiat and design
was paper handed, clasped and free
in solemn chant and bitter rhyme.

ALL MY FAVOURITE SHOWS

I can't remember all my favourite shows.
Just snatches of the opening songs remain.
The rest was worn through slowly by the pain
and lost. My past is ragged, faintly glows

and moans, and shuffles off into the night.
I can't remember whole years back in school,
just elbows out of cars, scum on the pool.
But I remember bird eyes catching light,

the place where red and black ants fought a war,
the drowned duck's grave, where grass fades into moss,
and mushrooms sprout, and spread their hats, and toss
out curls of smoke – ten thousand tiny spores.

And if I plant them in my mulched up years,
they'll grow up fine, well-watered by my tears.

FLOWERS

I like tiny little flowers,
not the great rich sprays in the breeze
but the shy ones, tucked into corners of trees
and the stone walls of rooms where we shag for hours.

Not marigolds. Roses, forgot and blown
and purple pink, more smell than round perfect buds
and the funk of seaweed and crabs and mud
on the beach where we find ourselves whole and alone.

I like flowers they call weeds,
catching paper in cracks between pavements and houses,
the silent beliefs held by long married spouses,
the passion and hope, wonder, terrible deeds

brought to critical mass by potential and power
and the small, forgotten leaves.

THE ASS OF MY ANXIETY

I wish my anxiety had an ass
so I could dress it in cute tops and jeans,
and we'd go out, pretend we were the queens
of life. We'd curse. We'd step down on the gas

and throw our mighty curves hard into gear.
We'd laugh and scream and know we were the best.
In freezing cold we'd walk out, brightly dressed
in clothes the world forgets this time of year,

the sequins, feathers, silks of summer's light.
I wish my anxiety had a voice,
some ears to hear, a mind, the gift of choice.
I'd make it see its glory and its might –

one day, catching a cold wind in its hair,
it finally would slow, and pause for air.

RED FLAGS

Beware the cheerful stranger bearing gifts.
He knew me – but, so soon! Meant he's a cad.
He wormed inside and tore my home to bits.
He spat, You're turning me into my dad.

Already left four times, so I'll go back.
Trouble, my mum said. Bitch. I'll prove her wrong.
He'll straighten out if I cut him some slack.
I've had to put away my favourite songs.

He liked me best when I was sick in bed.
I found a burner phone zipped in his coat.
He told me once, I'll miss you when you're dead.
He texted me his girlfriend's tits, to gloat.

He swapped his ring for molly at a rave.
At three am, he curled upon my grave.

THE DAY

Every one of us has the day when her heart hardens.
Every one of us, as much human as a statue is,
criss-crossed lines caulked on a cracked phiz,
bleached out and broken in the fire of a thousand pardons.

Every one of us, one day, sets, turns hard, away.
You can layer on and on the shiny coats of wax,
take gold solder, burn routes for lines of attack,
dry out the insides, glaze caverns and footsoles grey.

One day, maybe part through a story or a plea,
everything stops. Cries for help crystallise in the throat,
form a perfect cast of dreams mumbled, debates, frantic
votes.
It's nice to hold still, not to feel or see

or breathe, but only to nod and raise the oar
and tip over the waterfall, and pour.

IRIS

I would make a poor iris, basking in the sun,
rippling flags and scent bombs, luring insects deeper:
pinnacle of striving roots and nets of fungus,
wind and water, vitamins and salts, once dusted, done.

Never thought I'd find you swimming in the garden,
speckled and descended swiftly, at strange angles,
scarred from quiet battles, swinging out of danger,
curving towards the ending, sweet years that remain.

I would make a poor koi, hiding under lilies,
hammered gold and ivory, sealed against the water,
teeth leapt up from bottom, seizing water oarsmen,
lapis inlaid dragonfly plucking out my daughters.

Before I was human, I wished I were a lamb,
or a pony, or a sheepdog, bright and filled with purpose,
bounded by drystone walls, infinitely placid,
voices joined in sorrow, never reaching further.

How did I arrive from velvet wriggling frogspawn,
built of broken glass, cracked beads, discovered feathers,
daughter of quicksilver, made of rusted clockwork
all the pike-hung near-deaths, flapping silken banners?

Crystal fell from pocket, shining at the castle,
rainbow thin inclusions radiating sunlight.
I would make a poor gate, cleaving wind and water,
fire, smoke and whispers, worn by generations.

Peering into split rocks, looking for the planners,
drawing spines and jawbones out of dirt and chaos,
cast in bronze and copper, breath in beeswax candles.
I would make a poor mountain, grey and green and dun.

Every mother bore us, eyes askew, chins tilted,
raised in isolation, lacking common language.
Absent from the stories, spelled only in damage,
we would make poor priestesses, wan and drained of blood.

Walking over gravel past a field of bluebells,
path for carts dividing lambs and woolly mothers,
golden sun fades slowly, baby bleating loudly,
waiting for the answer: sadly, there is none.

I just saw a magpie drinking from the pond.
Blood of baby robins speckling pinfeathers,
smashing shells on pavements, heckling pacing tomcats.
I would make a poor witch, broke my magic wand.

GIGS FOR AUTISM

How I talk.
Old beats in my head, in my breath and walk,
songs I've hummed all day for hours
burst into riots of leaves, thorns and flowers.

How I talk.
Say fuck it to a gig next week
and blotched red apples of cheeks.
I'll throw the slap on. How I sing:

incantations of death,
secrets drawn in a maze,
no answer to threats, the fence
and the wheat fields whisper for days.

How I move in the night.
Nobody can hear me,
cats yowling, shy foxes fear me and scatter,
lamps go out one by one.

Then the darkness curls in, and I run
down the street, dizzy and mad as a hatter.

HELLO

I would say hello to you, but if
I called out, and you didn't answer, I'd
be fretful, and my anxious heart adrift
would wander into rocky shallows, wide

of any navigation point, recurse
on every nuanced syllable, and fret
that I'd offended – carelessly – or worse
that in my haste, I'd get my papers wet

and crumbling into pulp, I couldn't parse
the intricate conditions of my hail
and haplessly I'd fall right upon my arse
before the winds had lifted every sail –

instead I'll flit by windows in a blink
and pierce the hull, and watch it slowly sink.

THE BARE BONES OF MY FUCKS

Behold, the field in which I grow my fucks:
as barren, now, as Thatcher's mouldering grave.
The grey earth, a dry ditch, and two pink Crocs.
Sere tufts of crabgrass, sharp enough to shave.

High above, the sun is beating down,
And with it, the ground opens up its cracks,
All the gardeners spent the night in town,
And now they're crashed out on the empty sacks.

Their droning snores make harmony with flies,
While crickets chirp, and drink a hidden rill.
They lick their lips, rub dust out of their eyes.
Their yellow piss runs slowly down the hill.

And one by one, they drive off in their trucks.
Dust clouds, white glare. My field, so bare of fucks.

—

I tried to write my fucks down on a map,
And naturally, I drew two lines in war,
They shot, gassed, bayoneted, raped, and stabbed,
And died, half-mourned by creditors and whores.

And when the map was burned and streaked by soot,
All ruched up, torn, and bloodied by their fight,

A few brave fucks did make the climb on foot,
And broke their plane by struggling towards the light.

I was asleep, mired in a dream of fear,
I woke up to the boom of paper guns,
The burst of signal flares rattled my ears,
But I could see to snatch them, every one:

Caught, vermin, gasping, damning curséd luck,
Discarded, dying; stray sparks of my fucks.

—

Mine were the fucks that launched a thousand ships.
The rockets, coughing, hurled them to the stars.
The whole Earth watched their uneventful trip
And cheered as they touched safely down on Mars.

And as their robot arms unfurled like ferns
And gracefully assembled shining domes
Earth dutifully forgot what it had learned,
And picked up trifles closer in to home.

The ratings just kept slipping down the list.
The care packages – scrapped for lack of funds.
So slowly, they forgot that they were missed,
They planned it all, to gasp their last as one –

Burst suits, dried flesh, the Martian sun at dusk,
The howling wind; the bare bones of my fucks.

TALES TOLD BY THE GODS

If I become a cliff edge, without holds
for your hands, will you wander off, across
the plain? Or will you take your ax, and toss
it forward, hard? The steel, gleaming and cold

will hit the shale of me, and split the layers.
Your breath the winter wind, grind me to sand.
Between the blows, not all the thoughts and prayers
would raise a single blister on your hand.

Instead I'll let you carve steps in my back,
scoop out the vertebrae, insert your rods.
One day, we will be tales told by the gods.
Pasiphae wielded lust as an attack.

No herbs protect my faces, bitter stone.
I'll take no help, and be myself alone.

CORONA
INVOCATION

In the time of Corona
let me be brave.
Let dead comrades' ghosts haunt my ears with their words,
let old punk songs echo and pierce with new meanings,
the hospital corridors, shining and clean:
God save the Queen.

In the time of Corona
let my words be kind,
as all the disaster films slowly come true.
Let the lips of the gossips turn brightest blue,
and let robins eat grubs from the silent spring graveyard:
turned earth, new.

In the time of Corona
let me forgive,
as long sought horizons slowly curve in.
The hatters are fashioning plague masks and beaks,
the old hatreds rotting in steady spring winds
as our heartbeats are sirens all sounding for weeks:
Let us live.

ANGER, REMEMBERED IN A SUNNY LANE

The magpies are calling across to each other,
one roof in shadow, the other in sun,
the echo that warns, exhorts brother to brother,
the terrain for more battles routed than won,

the grandmothers walking the dogs past the lane
where the rottweiler shies from the terrier's bark
and the tears leak out eyes from the old referred pain
and the gasps and heart pounding in midsummer dark

playing words back from long ago, longer than hate
in my old toddler's heart, just before it was cored
and convicted and sentenced, hung out on the slate
because someone was frightened, addicted and bored.

One day I will have enough courage to curse
but until then, the shivers, the nightmares and worse.

DYING

No, I won't lift the shroud up off your back
and wrap it round my neck to keep it warm,
won't slip between the fits, the cough that racks
and shakes the bed, that twists your shrunken form,

won't whisper awful secrets in your ears
when you can't do a thing about it – just
snap eyes wide open, fill them up with tears.
Truth roars up to the dam, ready to bust,

but I won't let it break: instead, the creek,
the grassy bank, boats nodding by the pier.
I'll help you settle, trying not to speak,
and take the oars, for you won't need to steer

into that strange and hazy golden glow,
and go, before my levees overflow.

A WOMAN'S RIGHT

No raised voice is automatic madness,
Truth is love, vita fidelis semper.
Oh, for a woman's right to lose her temper.

Understanding, weeps in bitter sadness,
fierce shadow, the shakes, titanic clangour.
Oh, for a woman's right to show her anger.

Take a risk, her face a mask of gladness,
Back curled round a pulsing core of terror.
Oh, for a woman's right to be in error.

Brightly smiling, standing at the checkout,
beans and nappies whisper, caveat emptor.
Oh, for a woman's right to lose her temper.

Scars from when she tried to stick her neck out,
shrivelled sacred heart, the songs that sang her.
Oh, for a woman's right to show her anger.

Acknowledgements

The poems *Siena, Corona Requiem, All My Favourite Shows* first appeared in the online magazine, Red Wedge.

Siena also appeared in *CoronaVerses: poems from the pandemic*, edited by Janine Booth

Iris first appeared in the *Wonderzoo anthology – Maybe we can meet when this shit is over.*

About the author

Margaret is a poet, copywriter and journalist based in Plymouth, Devon. Her articles have been published widely online, including in the Guardian, the New Statesman, Cosmopolitan, and Narratively. Her poems have appeared in Red Wedge and as part of WonderZoo's online anthologies. She is a member of the Etherpoems digital poetry collective.